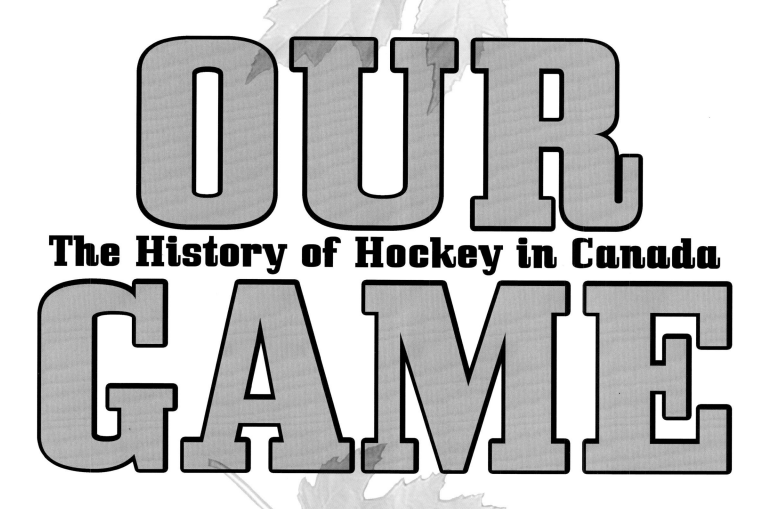

OUR
GAME

The History of Hockey in Canada

WRITTEN BY **Dave Stubbs**

ILLUSTRATED BY **Neal Portnoy**

Lobster Press ™

Respectfully dedicated to NHL legends Jean Béliveau, Elmer Lach, and Dickie Moore, superstars before I was born who became my heroes as we grew friendly many years later. To the late Stanley Cup champions Gerry McNeil, Kenny Mosdell, and Bernie Geoffrion, who generously shared with me their wonderful stories of hockey in the 1950s. To my friend, all-star defenceman Sheldon Souray. From skating on a frozen lake to playing in the NHL, he is living proof that hockey dreams can come true for any young Canadian. And finally, to my wife, Kathy, without whose support and espresso this book would not have been written.

– Dave Stubbs

I have devoted my entire adult life to sports, art, and children's charities. My parents supported my passion for sports and art, and taught me the importance of giving back to the community. Over the years, I have learned that any ability you're born with is enhanced by training, and practice, practice, practice. I dedicate this book to our youth, and to those who have a dream, live their dream, and pass along life's lessons, making the world a better place to live.

– Neal Portnoy

Our Game: The History of Hockey in Canada
Text © 2006 by Dave Stubbs
Illustrations © 2006 by Neal Portnoy

Published by Lobster Press™
1620 Sherbrooke Street West, Suites C & D
Montréal, Québec   H3H 1C9
Tel. (514) 904-1100 • Fax (514) 904-1101 • www.lobsterpress.com

Publisher: Alison Fripp
Editors: Alison Fripp & Meghan Nolan
Editorial Assistant: Molly Armstrong
Book Designer: Glenn Mielke
Production Manager: Tammy Desnoyers

We acknowledge the financial support of the Government of Canada through the Book Publishing Industry Development Program (BPIDP) for our publishing activities.

The Canada Council | Le Conseil des Arts
for the Arts | du Canada

We acknowledge the support of the Canada Council for the Arts for our publishing program.

Société de développement des entreprises culturelles
Québec

We acknowledge the support of the government of Québec, tax credit for book publishing, administered by SODEC.

Library and Archives Canada Cataloguing in Publication

Stubbs, Dave, 1957-
    Our game : the history of hockey in Canada / Dave Stubbs ; Neal Portnoy, illustrator.

(My Canada series)
ISBN-13: 978-1-897073-27-8 (bound)
ISBN-13: 978-1-897073-46-9 (pbk.)
ISBN-10: 1-897073-27-5 (bound)
ISBN-10: 1-897073-46-1 (pbk.)

    1. Hockey—Canada—History—Juvenile literature.
I. Portnoy, Neal, 1953- II. Title. III. Series: My Canada series (Montréal, Québec)

GV848.4.C3S88 2006   j796.962'0971   C2006-900724-1

Printed and bound in Canada.

On the cover, clockwise from top left: NHL stars Wayne Gretzky, Sidney Crosby, and Maurice (Rocket) Richard.

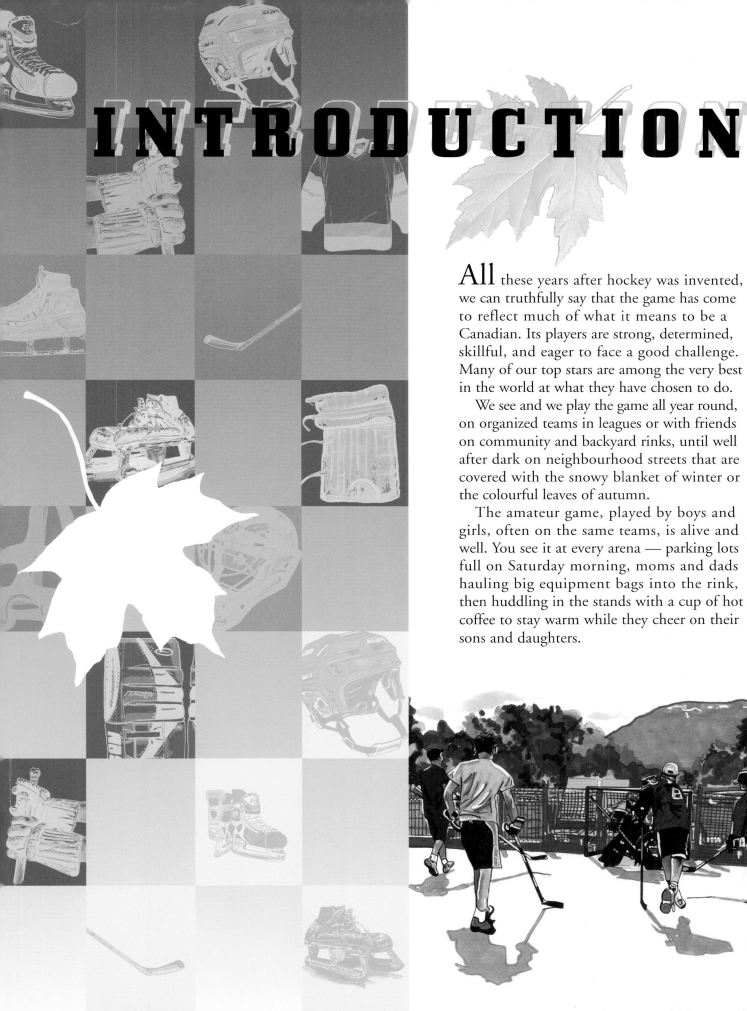

INTRODUCTION

All these years after hockey was invented, we can truthfully say that the game has come to reflect much of what it means to be a Canadian. Its players are strong, determined, skillful, and eager to face a good challenge. Many of our top stars are among the very best in the world at what they have chosen to do.

We see and we play the game all year round, on organized teams in leagues or with friends on community and backyard rinks, until well after dark on neighbourhood streets that are covered with the snowy blanket of winter or the colourful leaves of autumn.

The amateur game, played by boys and girls, often on the same teams, is alive and well. You see it at every arena — parking lots full on Saturday morning, moms and dads hauling big equipment bags into the rink, then huddling in the stands with a cup of hot coffee to stay warm while they cheer on their sons and daughters.

Canadian women's team star
Hayley Wickenheiser.
HOCKEY CANADA

Calgary Flames superstar
Jarome Iginla.
NHL

Young NHL star Sidney Crosby (left)
and Hall of Famer Mario Lemieux.
PITTSBURGH PENGUINS

Author's Note

If the transcontinental Canadian Pacific Railway of the 1880s helped to link people of this land with a steel thread, then hockey has done likewise with its stick and its puck.

The game knows no boundaries in Canada. While hockey first took root in the East, its popularity quickly swept it out to eager fans and players in the West. Today, hockey enjoys enormous popularity in every corner of our country.

In these pages, we'll explore the history of our national winter sport, from East to West, from South to North. Every village, town, and city in Canada has written its own chapter of hockey history. For every tale you read in *Our Game*, there are dozens more you'll learn — and experience — on your own.

— Dave Stubbs

Return to these same arenas late at night and you'll find leagues of "oldtimers," grown men age 60, or more, who love hockey too much to leave it behind.

We write songs, plays, and poems about hockey. It is celebrated in movies and books. We play it on frozen ponds and lakes, wearing the sweaters of our favourite teams, pretending we're Sidney Crosby, the Pittsburgh Penguins' young talent from Nova Scotia who many say will be the NHL's next huge star. Or maybe we're Wayne Gretzky, Jarome Iginla, Mats Sundin, Vincent Lecavalier, women's team stars Hayley Wickenheiser, Cassie Campbell, Kim St-Pierre, or a legend of long ago.

We keep scrapbooks and collect hockey cards, slap tennis balls against our garage doors, play it in video games and, sometimes, in our dreams.

The game has endured since the days before there was the internet, television, and even radio, through two world wars, a deadly flu, and the Great Depression.

In 1994, the elected leaders of our country finally recognized what everyone had known for a long time: that hockey is Canada.

With the National Sports of Canada Act, hockey was acknowledged by Parliament as this nation's official winter sport.

Like us, our government sees that hockey is a thread that runs from the Atlantic Ocean to the Pacific, a sport that links us as Canadians.

The Act does make us think about a great game and the many people who have made it so. It reminds us of street hockey and the Stanley Cup, of heroes the game has known for more than 100 years.

It leads us back to the days of long ago, to the recollections of our parents and grandparents, and into our libraries to discover more.

The National Sports of Canada Act reminds us of hockey's place in our culture and our hearts.

And because the game is woven into so much of our culture, studying the history of hockey is, in many ways, studying the history of Canada — with a glorious past and a very exciting future, just like the country it calls home.

This is the story of hockey in Canada.

SPORT CANADA

National Sports of Canada Act

CHAPTER N-16.7 (1994, c. 16)

[Assented to 12th May, 1994]

An Act to recognize hockey and lacrosse as the national sports of Canada

Her Majesty, by and with the advice and consent of the Senate and House of Commons of Canada, enacts as follows:

SHORT TITLE

1. This Act may be cited as the *National Sports of Canada Act*.

NATIONAL SPORTS OF CANADA

2. The game commonly known as ice hockey is hereby recognized and declared to be the national winter sport of Canada and the game commonly known as lacrosse is hereby recognized and declared to be the national summer sport of Canada.

The Department of Canadian Heritage SPORT CANADA

Hockey has often been about friendship. Here, Montreal Canadiens superstar Maurice (Rocket) Richard (standing) congratulates his team's goalie, Gerry McNeil, after a victory in the 1950s.
GERRY McNEIL COLLECTION

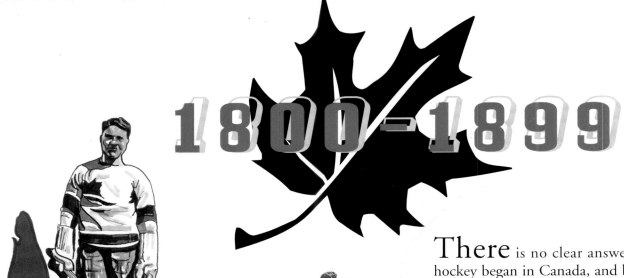

1800-1899

A woman ready to play in the 1800s.
HOCKEY: CANADA'S ROYAL WINTER GAME

How an early-day player would have dressed.

Hockey by Today's
Numbers

Amateur hockey in Canada has come a long way since the earliest games:

More than **4.5 million** Canadians of all ages are involved in the sport as players, coaches, officials, administrators, and volunteers.

2 million Canadians select hockey as their activity of choice.

1.5 million games are played every year.

535,000 Canadian boys, girls, men, and women were registered players in 2004–05 with Hockey Canada, the body that governs the operation of amateur (or minor) hockey.

More than **3,000** Canadian arenas are in operation.

Source: HOCKEYCANADA.CA, 2006

There is no clear answer as to where hockey began in Canada, and because of that, many people argue on behalf of one place or another.

British soldiers stationed in Canada were playing something that resembled hockey on frozen ponds in Kingston, Ontario, and Halifax and Dartmouth, Nova Scotia, around 1870. At the same time, in Montreal, McGill University students were playing on a downtown rink.

Windsor, Nova Scotia, and Deline, in the Northwest Territories, say they have proof that hockey was born in their towns, with assorted records and documents contained in their libraries.

But most evidence suggests that hockey, as it is most commonly defined, was born in Montreal. An early form of the game is said to have been played on a rink there in February 1837, a match between teams called Les Canadiens and the Dorchesters.

Nearly 40 years later, McGill students played the first "real" hockey game, as far as history can tell, on March 3, 1875 at the downtown Victoria Ice Rink located between Stanley and Drummond Sts., just below Ste. Catherine St. W., in Montreal.

TIMELINE

1867
With Confederation, Canada becomes a country.

1898
Montreal Arena opens, and hockey is played inside.

1892
Dominion Hockey Challenge Cup — or Stanley Cup — arrives in Canada from England, where it was made.

1877
First hockey rules are published.

1879
Teams are reduced to seven players, from nine.

1880s
Games are divided into two 30-minute halves.

RULES

The earliest known photo of a hockey game in progress, on the campus of McGill University during the Montreal Winter Carnival of 1884.
ALEX HENDERSON, COURTESY OF McGILL ATHLETICS

The first known photo of a hockey team in uniform, the McGill University club, at Montreal's Crystal Palace Skating Rink on Feb. 28, 1881.
WILLIAM NOTMAN, COURTESY OF McGILL ATHLETICS

But these early games were hardly hockey as we know it today, beginning with the fact that eight or nine players were on the ice for each team, compared to six who play now, and that a ball, and later a wooden puck, was used in order to prevent injuries. Today, the puck is made of hard rubber that is vulcanized, or processed, to be made weatherproof.

In 1877, McGill players formed the first official team and, playing under rules published that day in the *Montreal Gazette,* defeated the Montreal Victorias 2-1, a team composed mainly of members of the Montreal lacrosse and football clubs.

North America's first official league, the Amateur Hockey Association of Canada, is said to have been formed in 1885 in Kingston, Ontario. A year after that, the association included teams from Ottawa, McGill, and three other teams from Montreal — the Amateur Athletic Association, the Crystals, and the Victorias.

All players were amateurs, that is, they were not paid a penny to play.

The 1877 Rules of Ice Hockey

The first published rules of hockey, as they appeared in the *Montreal Gazette* on January 31, 1877. (The word "Bully" refers to a faceoff.)

1. The game shall be commenced and renewed by a Bully in the centre of the ground. Goals shall be changed after each (goal scored).

2. When a player hits the ball, any one of the same side who at such moment of hitting is nearer to the opponents' goal line is out of play, and may not touch the ball himself, or in any way whatever prevent any other player from doing so, until the ball has been played. A player must always be on his own side of the ball.

3. The ball may be stopped, but not carried or knocked on by any part of the body. No player shall raise his stick above his shoulder. Charging from behind, tripping, collaring, kicking or shinning shall not be allowed.

4. When the ball is hit behind the goal line by the attacking side, it shall be brought out straight 15 yards, and started again by a Bully; but, if hit behind by any one of the side whose goal line it is, a player of the opposite side shall hit it out from within one yard of the nearest corner, no player of the attacking side at that time shall be within 20 yards of the goal line, and the defenders, with the exception of the goal-keeper, must be behind their goal line.

5. When the ball goes off at the side, a player of the opposite side to that which hit it out shall roll it out from the point on the boundary line at which it went off at right angles with the boundary line, and it shall not be in play until it has touched the ice, and the player rolling it in shall not play it until it has been played by another player, every player being then behind the ball.

6. On the infringement of any of the above rules, the ball shall be brought back and a Bully shall take place.

7. All disputes shall be settled by the Umpires, or in the event of their disagreement, by the Referee.

Facts on the Fly

Stanley's Trophy: Then and Now

The Stanley Cup, first called the Dominion Hockey Challenge Cup, is the most cherished award in professional hockey, presented each year to the champion of the National Hockey League.

The trophy has changed a great deal since it was made in England in 1892, then just a small bowl 7 1/2 inches tall, 35 inches around, and 11 1/4 inches in diameter. Its base has been added to over the years in order to accommodate the names of the players on the winning teams, and today, the Stanley Cup is 35 1/4 inches tall and weighs 34 1/2 pounds.

There is no greater honour for an NHL player than to have his name included on the Cup. Generally, he must have played 41 or more games in the regular season to have his name appear. About 2,300 names are engraved in the bowl, on the collar beneath it, and on nine sterling silver bands.

In fact, there are three Stanley Cups today. The original bowl is on permanent display at the Hockey Hall of Fame in Toronto. A tall duplicate is awarded to the champion team and goes on the road for promotions, while a replica of that trophy is at the Hall of Fame when the duplicate Cup is travelling.

Beginning in 1936, players on Stanley Cup-winning teams were awarded a medal to commemorate their triumph. But since the late 1950s, miniature versions of the cup have been presented.

Hockey quickly received high-profile attention from Lord Stanley of Preston, the 16th Earl of Derby, Canada's sixth Governor-General. Lord Stanley so fell in love with the new game that he maintained a rink on the lawn of Rideau Hall, his residence in Ottawa. At least three of his children — a daughter, Isobel, and two sons — played with Ottawa teams.

In 1892, he had a silver bowl made in England at a cost of 10 guineas — $48.67, in Canadian money — and called it the Dominion Hockey Challenge Cup, to be awarded each year to the country's best amateur team.

Almost from the day he introduced his trophy, it was known as the Stanley Cup. The Montreal Amateur Athletic Association team was the first winner in 1893.

Until 1926, any team could challenge for the Cup, often with ridiculous results. In 1905, the champion Ottawa Silver Sevens team was challenged by the Dawson City Nuggets, a team from the Yukon. The

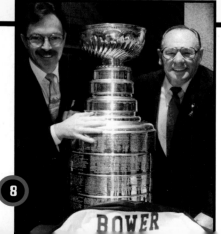

Author Dave Stubbs (left) with Toronto Maple Leafs goalie Johnny Bower and the Stanley Cup in 1993. The original Cup, called the Dominion Hockey Challenge Cup, was just the 7 1/2-inch tall silver bowl that sits atop the modern trophy in this photo.
AUTHOR'S COLLECTION

Women could hide the puck under their long skirts!

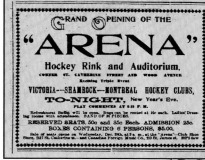

A newspaper ad invites fans to the opening of Montreal's grand new arena, and an artist's sketch shows spectators enjoying the action on December 31, 1898.
MONTREAL GAZETTE

Nuggets travelled 6,400 kilometres over 25 days — by dogsled to Alaska, then by boat to Vancouver, and by train to Ottawa — only to lose the two-game series against the Silver Seven by scores of 9-2 and 23-2. Ottawa's Frank McGee scored 14 goals in the second game. It was common for the Stanley Cup champion to be challenged for the trophy more than once per season in this manner, by any team that felt worthy. But by 1912, the tournament was played only once a year, at the end of the season.

Men and women cheered the early champions, as they do today. But from the beginnings of hockey, women were more than simply spectators. They, too, were forming their own teams, the first in 1894 at Queen's University in Kingston called the Love-Me-Littles.

Within two years, there would be women's teams at McGill in Montreal and in the Ottawa Valley, and more scattered from coast to coast toward the turn of the century.

And women had an advantage not enjoyed by the men — they played in long skirts, which goalies would spread out in front of the net to stop shots, and forwards would use to hide the puck when they stickhandled.

The Fan Experience

Until nearly the turn of the 20th century, hockey was played mostly outdoors. But on New Year's Eve 1898, the Montreal Arena was opened, not far from where the famous Montreal Forum would open on November 29, 1924.

A general-admission ticket to the Arena cost 25 cents, or 50 cents for a reserved seat. For $5, you could have a fancy private box, which would hold you and five friends. If you were cold at the Arena, you could rent a fur rug for your legs, big enough for two people, for a dime. And between periods, fans didn't munch on hot dogs and chips and drink pop or beer, as they do today. Instead, they were treated to a roast-beef buffet.

The new building held 7,000 spectators, one-third as many as Montreal's Bell Centre, which replaced the aging Forum in 1996.

The Arena, the home rink for the Montreal Canadiens and Montreal Wanderers, burned down on January 2, 1918. Sadly, the Wanderers team also collapsed, never to play again.

The Canadiens then played in the Jubilee Arena and Mount Royal Arena before moving into the Forum, the home address for 22 of the team's 24 Stanley Cup victories.

Facts on the Fly

The Hockey Net

It was around the turn of the 20th century that a simple invention proved to be one of the most useful in hockey: the goal net.

Frank Stocking, a Quebec goaler, was weary of all the disputed goals, scored (or not) between poles stuck in the ice. So, around 1900, Stocking and fellow goalie Charles Scott strung some netting between the posts and had their net approved by the Amateur Hockey Association of Canada for use.

Though Stocking and Scott's invention has been improved upon over the past century, it remains remarkably true to its earliest design. Players and fans liked that the net settled disputed scores, though goalies now couldn't claim the puck had missed the goal.

Chicago goalie Lorne Chabot guards the net in the 1930s. Chabot was born in 1900, the year the net was invented.
LIBRARY AND ARCHIVES CANADA

Amateur leagues continued to crop up throughout Canada, though players of that time gave little thought to making hockey a career. But that changed in 1904 with the creation of the International Professional Hockey League — hockey's first pro league, based in the northeast United States.

The IPHL lasted only three years, and was replaced in 1910 by the National Hockey Association (NHA), which was headquartered in Montreal and had teams in Quebec and Ontario. In 1911, the Vancouver-based Pacific Coast Hockey Association (PCHA) was born, with teams in British Columbia and the U.S. states of Washington and Oregon.

Amateur teams still flourished in Canada and the U.S., but the public was falling in love with the professional game. Both the NHA and the PCHA believed they offered hockey at its best, and in fact the champions of each association would meet to play for the Stanley Cup.

Professional team owners were mostly rich businessmen who also ran other companies. Many found the idea of owning clubs in the popular new sport too good to resist, and a team was something to show off to their friends.

TIMELINE

1901
Marconi receives a transatlantic radio message in St. John's, Newfoundland.

1909
Montreal Canadiens, pro hockey's oldest team, are founded.

1905
Montreal Westmount goalie Frank Brophy scores a goal.

1900
The goal net is introduced.

1907
If a player is injured in the first half of a game, he is permitted to rest for 10 minutes. He cannot be replaced by a healthy player. The other team plays with one man less.

1902
Teams are fined $10 if a game starts late. Players were sometimes delayed by weather or broken trains.

RULES

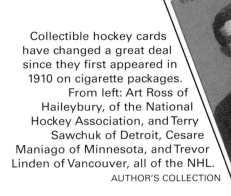

Collectible hockey cards have changed a great deal since they first appeared in 1910 on cigarette packages. From left: Art Ross of Haileybury, of the National Hockey Association, and Terry Sawchuk of Detroit, Cesare Maniago of Minnesota, and Trevor Linden of Vancouver, all of the NHL.
AUTHOR'S COLLECTION

1911

1951

1970

2003

However, teams came and went in professional hockey's early days. Some clubs were thriving and others were collapsing when their owners either ran out of money or simply lost interest in the game. The PCHA was down to just two teams by 1924, the Victoria Cougars and Vancouver Maroons, and they left to join the Western Hockey League. This was a young pro league operating in the Prairies during the 1920s, the first teams based in Edmonton, Calgary, Regina, and Saskatoon. In 1918, the NHA had also collapsed because members of its most popular team, the 228th Battalion, had been called into World War I action. The league also fell apart because team owners feuded bitterly over how their league should be run.

But a year before the NHA folded, a great new league was born in Montreal. It was called the National Hockey League, and it would change the game forever.

The great Ottawa Senators goaler Percy LeSueur, a Stanley Cup winner before the NHL was established.

Facts on the Fly

Hockey Cards

Today's serious collectors need to go all the way back to 1910 to find the first appearance of what is now a very popular hobby: hockey trading cards.

But they weren't sold in foil packs, with checklists and limited-edition cards. The first cards, from 1910 to 1913, were printed on cigarette packages, without today's shiny coating and detailed statistics. Kids relied on their parents to get their cards.

Other cards followed during the 1920s, produced by dairies, newspapers, and candy and chewing-gum companies. From 1934 to 1967, the St. Lawrence Starch Company of Port Credit, Ontario, would send fans a black and white picture of their favourite player in exchange for a paper collar found on metal tins of Bee Hive Corn Syrup.

Still a wider variety of cards appeared in the early 1950s, after World War II. The hobby began to really grow in 1951 with the first Parkhurst set, and soon other companies were printing their own cards.

Today, companies pay large sums of money to the NHL Players' Association for the right to put the photos of players on their cards.

1910-1919

Facts on the Fly

Rule Changes

The following rule changes accompanied the creation of professional hockey.

1911 Games are now divided into three 20-minute periods, allowing players a little more rest during a game. It was normal for a team to use the same players for an entire game, with substitutions used only in case of injury.

1914 Referees begin to drop the puck on face-offs, rather than place the puck on the ice. This was thought to give both players an equal chance to gain possession of the puck for their teams.

1918 Goalies are allowed to fall to the ice to make a save. Until now, the rules had prohibited this, as officials feared a goalie would simply lie on the ice in front of his net for an entire game, making it difficult for players who couldn't lift the puck with their shot.

1919 Forward passing is allowed between blue lines, adding more speed to a game which used to move up the ice side to side.

The new five-team National Hockey League was formed in 1917, absorbing much of the collapsed NHA. The NHL had the Montreal Canadiens and the Wanderers, the Quebec Bulldogs, the Ottawa Senators, and the new league's first Stanley Cup champions, the Toronto Arenas, who in 1919 were renamed the St. Patricks and, in 1927, the Toronto Maple Leafs.

With the NHL, a new era was dawning. Nearly 80 years before Canada's elected politicians voted it so, hockey already was Canada's national winter sport, and nearly every player was Canadian.

Owners of NHL teams were more organized than the men who had run clubs in the NHA, now shut down, and PCHA, soon to disappear. They knew that they had to operate their teams as a business if the game were to survive.

Lester Patrick not only was an important executive in the PCHA and NHL, he also played a game in goal at age 44 in the 1928 Stanley Cup finals for the New York Rangers, as an emergency replacement for the injured Lorne Chabot.

But great misery was just around the corner. The Spanish Influenza swept North America in 1919, a devastating illness that in 1918 and 1919 killed between 20 and 40 million people around the globe and infected one-fifth of the world's population. Montreal Canadiens defenceman Joe Hall, stricken with the illness, was hospitalized in Seattle during the championship final. Other players were much too sick from the virus to play. The series was abandoned, and Hall died a few days later.

This tragedy prevented the Stanley Cup from being awarded in 1919, the only time this happened until the NHL's labour dispute of 2004–05 cancelled the entire season.

Hockey survived this terrible blow, however, and entered the 1920s with teams in both Canada and the U.S., and became an even greater part of Canadians' lives. A night at a professional hockey game was a big event — men wore suits, women wore their fur coats, and lucky children got to stay up past their bedtime — and teams now had more and more fans.

The PCHA had teams in Washington and Oregon, making professional hockey a truly international game. Women's hockey was now played on both sides of the border, too, with Canadian and American teams playing a tournament in Cleveland, Ohio, in 1916.

CANADIENS WILL RETAIN THE CUP

Were Holders of Stanley Cup When Present Series Started — Hall and McDonald Seriously Ill

Although there is no precedent or ruling to cover the extraordinary situation now existing in regard to the Stanley Cup, it is likely that Can-

WORLD'S HOCKEY SERIES CANCELLED

Seven of the Canadiens and Owner George Kennedy Stricken With "Flu"

Seattle, April 1 —Definite and final

Headlines in Montreal newspapers announced the cancellation of the 1919 Stanley Cup playoffs.

Canadiens defenceman Joe Hall died from the Spanish Influenza.

TIMELINE

1914
World War I begins in Europe.

1917
National Hockey League is established.

1919
Flu outbreak cancels Stanley Cup playoffs.

1920-1929

The gold medal, team photo, and champion's pennant of the Winnipeg Falcons, winners of the first Olympic ice-hockey tournament played at Antwerp, Belgium, in 1920. A *Montreal Herald* story announced the victory.
MEDAL, PENNANT: COURTESY BRIAN JOHANNESSON; TEAM PHOTO: AUTHOR'S COLLECTION

Hockey wasn't the only thing that attracted the attention of sports fans during the 1920s. The modern Olympic Games had been founded in 1896 by the French baron Pierre de Coubertin, and in the 1920s, Canadians thrilled to the Olympic performances of the country's best amateur athletes.

It's little wonder, given its growing popularity in Europe, that hockey would be welcomed into the Olympics as well.

Amateur players (unlike today, no pros were allowed in the Olympics) from seven countries — Canada, Belgium, Czechoslovakia, France, Sweden, Switzerland, and the United States — were invited to participate in the Games of the VII Olympiad in Antwerp, Belgium, in 1920. Hockey was played at the Summer Olympics, of all things, because the first Winter Olympics would not officially be held for another four years.

The Winnipeg Falcons represented Canada and proved unbeatable, winning the six-team tournament by outscoring opponents 29-1 in their three games.

Canada also prevailed at the first Olympic Winter Games in 1924 in Chamonix, France. The Toronto Granites wore the Maple Leaf and also won the gold medal. In five games, the Granites outscored their opponents 110-3.

NEWS WHEN IT'S NEW

Yesterday was not only a Blue Monday for K. O. Clay, but a Black and Blue Monday.

Harry, The

FALCONS WIN FIRST TITLE AT OLYMPICS IN HOCKEY VICTORY

Canadians Out-class Europe in Hockey and Sweden's only goal in the Final Game Was a Gift — Swedes Could Skate Fast but Didn't Know the Game

TIMELINE

1926
Legendary goalie Georges Vézina dies of tuberculosis.

1923
Canadian National Railways is formed.

1922
Ottawa Senators play NHL's first-ever tie game, against Toronto.

1921
Minor penalties are now two minutes, reduced from three.

1926
Nets are made a standard six feet wide by four feet high, and fastened to the ice.

1927
Teams change ends after each period.

1929
Ice is now divided into defending, neutral, and offensive zones. Offside rule is introduced.

RULES

At home in Canada, hockey was never more popular, thanks in part to stars like Montreal Canadiens goaler Georges Vézina, who in 1918 recorded the NHL's first shutout, blanking the Toronto Arenas 9-0.

But there was much sadness in the NHL on March 26, 1926, when Vézina died from the lung disease tuberculosis. That autumn, to honour his memory, the Canadiens donated the Vézina Trophy to the NHL, which has been awarded every year since to the league's best goalie.

The NHL was growing quickly. In 1926, the league expanded to include 10 teams, divided into Canadian and American divisions, and fans were flocking to games in huge numbers. The NHL didn't begin keeping attendance figures until the 1926–27 season, and that year, 1,119,961 fans attended 220 league games — an average of 5,090 people for each game. Today's Montreal Canadiens have more than four times that number for each of their home games, but the arenas in the NHL's early days were much smaller compared to the modern buildings.

Canadiens goaler Georges Vézina, for whom the Vézina Trophy is named.

The Vézina Trophy

Former owners of Vézina's team created and donated the Vézina Trophy to the NHL, and it was awarded for the first time following the 1926–27 season. Fittingly, it was won for the first three times by Canadiens' George Hainsworth.

Until the 1981–82 season, the goalkeeper(s) of the team allowing the fewest number of goals during the regular season was awarded the trophy. But since then, NHL team general managers have awarded it to "the goalkeeper adjudged to be the best at his position."

Other major individual NHL trophies awarded to players:

Hart Memorial Trophy: most valuable to his team
Art Ross Trophy: regular season's leading points-scorer (goals and assists)
Calder Memorial Trophy: outstanding rookie
James Norris Memorial Trophy: outstanding defenceman
Frank J. Selke Trophy: outstanding defensive forward
Lady Byng Memorial Trophy: most gentlemanly player
Williams M. Jennings Trophy: goalie(s) on one team with fewest goals against
Conn Smythe Trophy: most valuable in the playoffs
Jack Adams Award: outstanding coach
Bill Masterton Memorial Trophy: outstanding perseverance, sportsmanship, and dedication
King Clancy Memorial Trophy: outstanding leadership on and off the ice
Maurice (Rocket) Richard Trophy: leading scorer in the regular season (goals only)

Toronto Maple Leafs goalie Walter (Turk) Broda with the Vézina Trophy, which he won twice in the 1940s.
HOCKEY ONLINE

Dollars and Cents

It costs much more to go to an NHL game today compared to many years ago. Of course, in those days, players and fans earned much less money, and products, goods, and services cost less, too. This increase, over time, is called inflation.

People used to be able to go see the best NHL players for as little as 25 cents for a ticket that let them stand behind the net, high in the stands. The best seat in many arenas in the 1920s and '30s, not long after the NHL was formed, cost about $3.

Compare that to the average ticket prices for Canada's NHL teams during the 2005–06 season. The figure in parentheses is the average ticket price in 1993–94, when the Team Marketing Report newsletter began keeping track of this information.

Vancouver: $54.08 ($41.03) **Toronto:** $49.23 ($35.68)
Montreal: $47.58 ($28.20) **Edmonton:** $43.46 ($20.84)
Calgary: $40.92 ($22.79) **Ottawa:** $40.76 ($36.83)

The Royal Victoria College women's team, representing McGill, who lost to the University of Toronto for the Canadian women's collegiate title in 1921.
McGILL ATHLETICS

In 1927–28, the most expensive ticket for an NHL game was $3.50, which is what you'd pay to watch the New York Rangers, New York Americans, or Chicago Blackhawks. But at Toronto's Mutual Street Arena, you could get in the door to watch the action for just 25 cents — provided you didn't mind standing the whole game.

And it wasn't just the men who were proving that hockey could be played at a high level. The University of Toronto women's team defeated McGill to win the 1921 intercollegiate title, the first of their 11 championships.

Broadcaster Foster Hewitt brought hockey to millions of Canadians, first on radio, then on television.
HOCKEY ONLINE

Hockey Comes to the
Radio

In the 1920s, before the invention of television, fans followed hockey games after the fact through reports in newspapers and on the radio news. So imagine the excitement on March 14, 1923, when Pete Parker made hockey's first live radio broadcast in Regina, Saskatchewan, describing a Western League game between the Edmonton Eskimos and the Regina Capitals.

Eight days later, Toronto newspaper reporter Foster Hewitt broadcast a minor-league matchup he announced through a telephone, live on Toronto radio.

This led the way for more and more games to be broadcast, and soon Canadians from coast to coast would be gathered around their big radios, listening to Hewitt's voice.

He would later become even more famous for his announcing work on *Hockey Night in Canada* television broadcasts, and for being the first man to shout, "He shoots! He scores!" to declare a goal.

1930-1939

If hockey had been growing in the 1920s, it boomed in the 1930s. More and more fans filled the arenas for games, despite the financial pain many were feeling at the time.

The 1929 crash of the stock market had emptied the bank accounts and ruined the lives of millions. Hockey, like all businesses, felt the effects. For a variety of reasons, including the stock market crash, three franchises — the Pittsburgh Pirates, the Montreal Maroons, and the Ottawa Senators — hadn't the money to keep playing, and they dropped out of the NHL during the Great Depression, or deep poverty, of the 1930s.

| WEATHER Gales, Rain | Montreal Herald. | HOME EDITION |

MONTREAL'S MODERN EVENING NEWSPAPER

116th YEAR No. 1 ★ ★ MONTREAL, THURSDAY, OCTOBER 24, 1929 C PRICE TWO CENTS

Panic Sweeps Country's Stock Markets

A stock market crash happens when there is a large, sudden drop in the value of shares of stock — or ownership — of companies in which ordinary people have invested their savings.

Fred (Cyclone) Taylor was a huge star on the PCHA's Vancouver Millionaires.

Facts on the Fly

Western Wins

The 1930s dawned without a Western Canada contender for the Stanley Cup.

The Pacific Coast Hockey Association (PCHA) had been founded in 1911 with the New Westminster Royals, Victoria Aristocrats, and the Vancouver Millionaires. Beginning in 1915, the champion of the PCHA played the champion of the National Hockey Association (NHA), the Eastern Canada league that would lead to the creation of the NHL, for the Stanley Cup.

The Western Canada Hockey League was formed in 1921, which brought about the end of the PCHA, and in 1925, the Victoria Cougars won the Stanley Cup. A Western Canada team would not again win the Cup until the Edmonton Oilers in 1984. The Oilers have won the Stanley Cup five times, while the Calgary Flames won in 1989.

Alberta teams were the NHL's powerhouse from 1984–90, winning the Cup six times in seven seasons.

TIMELINE

1930
Each player must now wear a number on his back.

1931
NHL formally recognizes an assist on a goal.

1932
If a goalie is penalized and must leave the ice, the coach may designate a substitute goalie.

1933
Every NHL rink must have a time clock.

1934
Penalty shot rule is introduced, allowing a player who had been fouled when "in a good scoring position" to take a free shot at the goaler from within a 10-foot circle, 38 feet from in front of the net.

1937
First icing rule introduced.

1939
World War II begins in Europe.

RULES

All-Star Game

The annual NHL All-Star Game is a chance for the league's best players to show off their skills. But the All-Star Game wasn't always played just for fun.

Three "all-star" games were played in the 1930s. The first, in 1934, raised money for the Toronto Maple Leafs' Ace Bailey, a star player whose career was ended by injury. Two more games were then held to benefit the families of two Montreal Canadiens — Howie Morenz, who died in 1937, and Albert (Babe) Siebert, who drowned in Lake Huron during a family beach trip in 1939.

The first "official" All-Star Game was held in 1947 in Toronto, with the Stanley Cup-champion Maple Leafs playing an NHL all-star team. The All-Star Game then became an annual event.

The format of the game has changed over the years, and today, fans play a large part in choosing the all-stars, voting for their favourite players. All-star weekend features a competition, which tests players in categories like shooting accuracy, puck control relay, fastest skater, hardest shot, and a breakaway relay.

It was a sad decade in other ways, too. Montreal Canadiens superstar Howie Morenz broke his leg during a game against the Chicago Blackhawks in 1937 and died in his sleep in a Montreal hospital six weeks later of a blood clot. He was only 34 years old.

Morenz was the heart and soul of the Canadiens, a player so fast on his skates that he was nicknamed the "Mitchell Meteor" and the "Stratford Streak" by the two Ontario towns that claimed he was their native son.

The entire NHL was heartbroken by his death. Tens of thousands of people attended Morenz's funeral, held March 11, 1937, at centre ice of the Montreal Forum. Sportswriters later voted Morenz as Canada's greatest male athlete of the first half of the 20th century.

By now, the look of hockey was beginning to change. Players were required to wear numbers on their uniforms. Until this time, fans and sometimes the coaches had to guess who was on the ice. In addition, Clint Benedict of the Montreal Maroons had briefly given goaltending a new face, wearing a primitive leather mask to protect his broken nose.

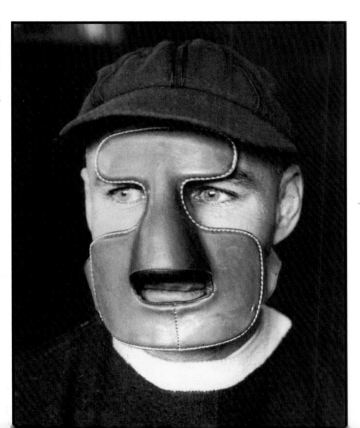

Clint Benedict of the Montreal Maroons was the first to wear a goalie mask in the NHL, using this one briefly in 1930 to protect a broken nose.
LIBRARY AND ARCHIVES CANADA

Montreal's Howie Morenz was voted Canada's greatest athlete of the first half of the 20th century, in any sport. His sudden death was a tragedy for all of hockey.

In the 1920s, rinks were cleared with long brooms. Twenty years later, men pushing shovels did the job.
LIBRARY AND ARCHIVES CANADA

And now, when a puck was deflected over the boards, fans would keep it for a souvenir instead of throwing it back. In fact, the puck often left the rink when it bounced off poor, chippy ice.

But an inventor named Frank J. Zamboni soon would have a cure for that.

The first Zamboni machine, the Model A, as it appeared in 1949.
COURTESY FRANK J. ZAMBONI CO. INC.

Some fun facts about the Zamboni machine:

● In 2001, a Zamboni machine, the 7,500th manufactured, was driven on a publicity trip from St. John's, Newfoundland, to Victoria, B.C. Travelling at about 14 km/h, the cross-Canada journey took about four months.

● By 2005, more than 8,000 machines had been delivered to rink operators around the world.

● When a Zamboni machine resurfaces a rink, it picks up about 3,300 kilograms of snow and leaves behind about 2,600 kg of water.

● The 21st machine built by Frank Zamboni, sold to the NHL's Boston Bruins in 1954, is on display at the Hockey Hall of Fame in Toronto, Ontario.

● And finally, to answer the question, "Why does a Zamboni machine have headlights?" Because it might be required to travel by road at night, as it did from St. John's to Victoria in 2001, and many leave their arena to dump the snow collection tank.

Facts on the Fly

Zamboni's Cool Machine

There's quite a history behind the world's most famous ice-resurfacing machine.

In 1939, Frank J. Zamboni of Eureka, Utah, built the huge, open-air Iceland Skating Rink in Southern California. He put a domed roof on the facility one year later because the hot sun and dry winds were making it difficult to maintain good artificial ice.

But it took three to five workers more than an hour to resurface the rink by pulling a scraper behind a tractor to shave the ice, before shovelling up the shavings, flooding the rink with water, and sweeping away the excess with squeegees, then finally applying another coat of water to finish the job.

In the early days of the NHL, men with huge brooms and buckets of water, then hoses, would do the same work. Later, they would pull, by hand, huge water drums to resurface a rink.

In March 1942, Frank Zamboni bought a tractor and began experimenting to find a way to do the job more efficiently. After seven years of work, his invention — the Model A Zamboni Ice Resurfacer — was working at the Iceland rink.

The machine has changed since that historic "Model A" was born in 1949, but its job remains the same — to scrape an ice rink, flood it with water, and smooth the water into a shiny, mirror finish.

Today, the company builds machines at a plant in California and in Brantford, Ontario, the hometown of hockey legend Wayne Gretzky. It costs between $10,000 and $150,000, depending on the size, and is driven — very carefully — around the ice by a member of an arena's maintenance staff.

A modern Zamboni machine of the 1990s, happy to be at work!
COURTESY FRANK J. ZAMBONI CO. INC.

A Great Canadian
Invention

You needn't play hockey on a rink, of course. You can play on a hand-held computer game, on your television, or on an air-hockey game at the arcade.

But long before the computer age, a Canadian named Donald Munro invented the table-hockey game, which was very popular for decades and is still played today.

In 1930, Munro came up with the idea of making a miniature rink with metal players attached to short spikes, who slid up and down the "ice" on steel rods to slap the puck at a metal goalie.

Some of Munro's first table-hockey games were sold in the 1939 Eaton's mail-order catalogue for about $5 — roughly the cost of a couple of pucks today.

One of the first table-hockey games, designed and built by Donald Munro of Hamilton, Ontario.
CLASSIC COLLECTIBLES

Women's hockey was going strong during this decade. The Rivulettes of Preston, Ontario, were nearly unbeatable, losing only two league games of the 350 they played through the 1930s.

But World War II changed the course of women's involvement in hockey. Because of the war, and the role women had to play, both in uniform and supporting the children of their husbands who went overseas to fight, women's hockey would largely disappear while they worked on the war effort. It took another 30 years for it to regain its ground.

The war would have a major impact on the NHL, too.

Facts on the Fly

The NHL's Longest Game

The fans at the Montreal Forum on March 24 and 25, 1936 witnessed the longest game played in NHL history.

It was a semifinal playoff game between the Montreal Maroons and Detroit Red Wings, and it was scoreless through three periods, then through five periods of overtime, until Detroit's Modere (Mud) Bruneteau scored the winner at 2:25 a.m. on March 25 — the morning after the action had begun — on Maroons goaler Lorne Chabot.

The game had lasted 176 minutes, 30 seconds, and some fans were sound asleep on the Forum benches when it finally ended. This is an NHL record that seems unlikely to ever be broken.

Early arena clocks were hard to figure out.
LIBRARY AND ARCHIVES CANADA

Margaret Cameron, dressed for action, prepares to make a big save.
McGILL ATHLETICS

By the 1942–43 season, the NHL was a six-team league: Montreal Canadiens and Toronto Maple Leafs in Canada, and Boston Bruins, Chicago Blackhawks, Detroit Red Wings, and New York Rangers in the United States.

In the early 1940s, many players on all six of these clubs — the "Original Six," as they were nicknamed — were called to serve their countries in World War II. This made room for new talent during a time when some of the most skilled players in hockey history were beginning to make their mark.

Some teams were badly hurt by the loss of players to the war effort. But others were planning for their future. The Canadiens found work for some of their players in wartime industries like ship- and aircraft-building and the manufacture of ammunition, which kept them at home instead of going overseas. These men worked these jobs by day, played hockey at night, and many went on to become established stars in the NHL.

Facts on the Fly

O Canada...

It wasn't until the 1946 season, perhaps as a symbol of pride following World War II, that the NHL officially declared that the national anthem of the home team must be played.

Today, both Canadian and U.S. anthems are heard at games featuring teams from the two countries.

At the beginning, the anthem was usually played by the arena organist, or on a record, with fans sometimes singing along. In Montreal, however, former army sergeant and opera singer Roger Doucet became famous for singing "O Canada" at the Forum in the 1970s.

In 2001, 20 years after Doucet died, Canadian astronaut Chris Hadfield heard the singer's version of "O Canada" in his space helmet as he walked in orbit outside the space shuttle, high above Newfoundland, working on the Canadian-made robotic Canadarm 2.

IT COSTS $135.75 TO EQUIP GOALIE

SUSPENDERS $1.25

SHOULDER PADS $11

BODY PAD $8.50

SWEATER $6

ELBOW PADS $6.50

GLOVES $10.75

PANTS $5.50

SHIN PADS $45

STICK $3.75

SOCKS $2.50

SKATES $35

Frank Brimsek of Boston Bruins shows what well-dressed hockey goalie is wearing... and what it costs.

Today, it costs about $6,000 to outfit an NHL goalie from his mask to his skates. In the 1940s, Boston's Frank Brimsek showed it cost a lot less.
COURTESY HOWARD McINTYRE

TIMELINE

1948
Goalie Emile Francis wears a baseball-style mitt in nets.

1945
World War II ends; 42,000 Canadian soldiers lost their lives.

1942
Bep Guidolin, age 16, becomes the youngest NHL player ever.

1940
NHL rules that ice must be flooded between periods to improve the quality of the ice.

1945
Goal lights are used for the first time.

1946
Referees begin using hand signals.

RULES

Hockey Hall of Fame

More than 5,700 men have played in the NHL since the league was founded in 1917. But it was only in 1943 that discussions began to create a Hockey Hall of Fame to celebrate the greatest names in the game.

The first members were inducted in 1945, and in 1961 an exhibition hall was finally opened in Toronto, with artifacts and exhibits displayed to the public. Eleven men were inducted in 1945, including Howie Morenz and Georges Vézina of the Canadiens, Ottawa's Frank McGee, Winnipeg-native goalie Chuck Gardiner of the Chicago Blackhawks, and Lord Stanley of Preston.

Today, there are more than 340 Honoured Members in the "hockey shrine," as it's called, recognizing the greatest players, builders — the men who helped shape the sport and the teams, such as coaches, managers, team owners, and executives — and referees and linesmen. More are added each year, voted in by a committee that reviews suggestions made by themselves or the public. As well, more than 75 hockey writers and broadcasters are recognized for their work in promoting the sport.

The Hall of Fame first opened in a building on the grounds of Toronto's Canadian National Exhibition, near the shores of Lake Ontario. It was replaced in 1993 by a new and improved Hall that was opened in the heart of downtown Toronto.

The Hall boasts hundreds of exhibits, hands-on displays and games, and, in its resource centre, thousands of documents, books, magazines, and photographs that are available for viewing and study.

More than 500,000 people visited the Hall in 1993, and today it is one of Toronto's leading tourist attractions.

The great all-around player Gordie Howe was nicknamed "Mr. Hockey."

It was in 1943 that the league introduced an important new rule to speed up the game. Until now, a player had to carry the puck across his own blue line. But for the 1943–44 season, the rule was changed to allow a pass up to the middle of the rink, which would be marked by a new red centre-ice line.

Coming up with Detroit during this decade was young Gordie Howe of Floral, Saskatchewan, a quiet but rugged player who enjoyed a 25-year NHL career beginning in 1946. Howe, who earned the nickname "Mr. Hockey," played 1,924 games, including playoffs, and scored 869 goals. Until Wayne Gretzky came along in the 1980s, he was the greatest all-around player hockey had ever seen.

Chicago goalie Chuck Gardiner, here in his all-star uniform, was among the first group of players elected to the Hockey Hall of Fame in 1945.
HOCKEY ONLINE

The Canadiens' Punch Line of the 1940s was one of the most feared lines of all time. Centreman Elmer Lach stands between his wingers, Maurice (Rocket) Richard (left), and Toe Blake.
ELMER LACH COLLECTION

The Hockey Hall of Fame plaque that immortalizes Rocket Richard.

But the athlete who perhaps stood out the most in the 1940s and the '50s was Montreal's legendary Maurice (Rocket) Richard, an intense right-winger who earned his nickname for his explosive force.

The Rocket played alongside his centreman, Elmer Lach, and opposite left-winger Toe Blake, who later would win eight Stanley Cups coaching the Canadiens. Together they were known as the "Punch Line" because they had great goal-scoring "punch." During the 1944–45 season, Richard scored 50 goals in 50 games, the first player to do so.

While the Canadiens' Punch Line filled the net, the Toronto Maple Leafs were the most consistently successful team through the decade, winning the Stanley Cup five times with the help of players like Syl Apps, Ted (Teeder) Kennedy, Bill Barilko, and roly-poly goalie Turk Broda.

Toronto Maple Leafs captain Ted (Teeder) Kennedy, his teammates, and team owner Conn Smythe accept the 1949 Stanley Cup from NHL president Clarence Campbell (right).
AUTHOR'S COLLECTION

Toronto Leafs Win Third Successive Stanley Cup

Montreal Gazette, April 17, 1949

continued on page 28

The EVOLUTION of AMATEUR & COMMUNITY HOCKEY

Hockey was played purely for fun long before the NHL was born.

In Canada, the game that was first enjoyed on frozen ponds and rivers — community hockey — was often called "shinny," a word derived from the 17th-century Scottish game "shinty," in which two teams of 12 players tried to hit a small ball into the goal of their opponent.

Almost anyone who could skate — mostly boys and men, but sometimes girls and women, too — joined shinny teams that represented companies, towns, churches, even prisons. Often, these teams would travel to other towns and challenge similar clubs, with nothing at stake but their pride.

Shinny is still played on Canadian rinks, though it's better known as "pick-up hockey," with teams chosen from among the players who show up at an outdoor rink. It's often on these rinks, and in arenas, that the love of the game begins. In fact, people often play hockey before they've learned to skate, and many enjoy ball-hockey games year-round.

A devotion grows in organized minor hockey as the player gets older — from the novice age group — about eight years old, through atom, peewee, bantam, midget, and junior, into later teens and, sometimes, in college or university.

While the boys and men used to completely dominate organized hockey, women's interest in the sport has grown significantly. In younger age groups, girls often play on the same team as boys.

That trail was blazed in the 1950s, when nine-year-old Abigail Hoffman of Toronto could find no girls' team on which to play. So she cut her hair, called herself Ab Hoffman and registered in a boys' league, and was even an all-star defenceman on a junior boys' team in St. Catharines, Ontario, before she was discovered to be a girl. She kept playing, and in 1982, she helped create the first national women's championship in Canada. Today, the Abby Hoffman Cup is awarded to the annual winner of the tournament.

Many girls and women have come to learn what Hoffman knew: hockey is a great game to play. In 1994–95, there were 19,050 female players registered in Canada; in 2004–05, that number had more than tripled, to 60,250.

It's clear the NHL is only the tip of the hockey iceberg. For more than a century, Canadians have handed down hockey traditions in their families and communities. It's this love and respect of our national winter sport — at all levels of play — that keeps hockey healthy.

The Road to the NHL from Amateur Ranks

For every one who plays in the NHL, there are thousands who play hockey just for the love of the game, fun, and for fitness. But it's in community hockey, or casual games of shinny, where many of the best players in the world take their first strides toward a career in the NHL — professional hockey's best league.

One such example is Sheldon Souray, a native Métis and one of a dozen aboriginal Canadians who has played in the NHL. Souray learned to skate and play hockey on Fishing Lake, Alberta, shooting pucks into snowbanks before his parents enrolled him in minor hockey in Edmonton. The defenceman was drafted into the NHL by New Jersey in 1994, and in 2000 was traded to Montreal.

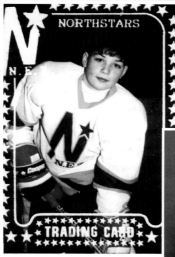

The odds were greatly against Souray, as they are today against anyone who hopes to play in the NHL. Players must have exceptional talent, supportive parents, excellent coaches, and be willing to work long hours on improving their skills in every area — while keeping good grades at school.

Sometimes, players must be prepared to move away from home at a young age to play on a junior or university team where they can be "scouted" or seen by men who are hired by NHL clubs to identify the talent that they believe could one day best help their teams. For the select few who are chosen, playing in the NHL is the dream of a lifetime.

The NHL, with its central scouting bureau, grades junior-age talent in North America and Europe and ranks it on a long list. It's from this list that the NHL's 30 teams annually choose players like Sidney Crosby of Pittsburgh and Alexander Ovechkin of Washington, two of the league's most impressive rookies in 2005–06.

The "entry draft" is televised, and it can be an emotional moment when a player steps onto the stage and pulls on the sweater and cap of the team that's drafted him.

The player then usually returns to his junior team and moves up to a minor-pro club, part of the NHL team's "farm system," to further develop his skills. The dream is complete when he finally gets the call to play in the NHL.

SHELDON SOURAY
DEFENSEMAN • MONTREAL CANADIENS®

From top: Sheldon Souray, age eight, wearing his Evansdale (Edmonton) Maple Leafs minor-hockey sweater. At age 10, playing for the Evansdale Eagles. At age 11, on his first hockey card, with the North East (Edmonton) North Stars. At age 18, with the Tri-Cities Americans junior team in the Western Hockey League. At age 28, on his 2004–05 Canadiens NHL card.

The EVOLUTION of

Hockey equipment has evolved over the decades, just as the game has changed.

The Changing Face of the
Goalie

1927: Elizabeth Graham of Queen's University in Kingston, Ontario, wore a fencing mask to protect her face in collegiate games.

1930: Clint Benedict of the NHL's Montreal Maroons wore a piece of leather on his face to protect a broken nose (see page 18). But he tossed it off almost immediately when he started to play, unable to see properly.

1950s: Jacques Plante of the Montreal Canadiens, who gets the most credit for the mask, wore a fibreglass model in practice against the wishes of his coach, Toe Blake. He set an example for other goalies when he finally wore it in a game.

1973: Andy Brown of the Pittsburgh Penguins became the last NHL goalie to adopt wearing a mask.

Jacques Plante changed the face of goaltending forever when he wore this mask in a game on November 1, 1959.

Helmets

Since 1979, NHL players have had to wear helmets. Boston Bruins rookie George Owen is credited with being the first hockey player to wear one in the NHL in 1928, using the leather football helmet he wore at Harvard University.

Today, many players have eye-protecting visors on their hard, lightweight plastic helmets (such as the one seen here), and minor-hockey players are required to wear full masks to protect the entire face. They must wear these cages or visors through junior and college hockey, according to the rules.

Sweaters

Sweaters used to be made of wool (left), and they were heavy and smelly when they got wet. Now, they are synthetic (right) — they dry almost instantly, and are nearly indestructible.

Gloves

Barehanded players saw the benefits of gloves. "Gauntlets" (seen here), the early form of the gloves used today, began to appear around 1915.

HOCKEY EQUIPMENT

Pants

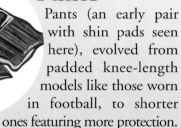

Pants (an early pair with shin pads seen here), evolved from padded knee-length models like those worn in football, to shorter ones featuring more protection.

Skates

In the late 1800s, skates were two pieces, sharp blades strapped or bolted to lace-up boots. In the 20th century, "tube skates" were introduced. Eventually, stainless steel blades were riveted onto leather boots (left).

Today, skates are made of many materials and are lightweight and strong (right).

Leg Pads

Early players didn't wear shin guards. At first, goalies wore leg pads designed for the British game of cricket, then heavy leather pads stuffed with horsehair and trimmed with felt. Before long, all players began to sew pads into their heavy woollen socks. By the 1960s, they were using tougher plastic models. Today, equipment has evolved with lightweight, space-age materials (as seen here in modern goalie pads) that protect players better than ever before.

Evolution of the Puck

Before the hard rubber puck was introduced to hockey, games were played with different objects, including rubber balls, frozen fruit, flattened tin cans, wooden pucks, and even frozen horse manure.

The high-bouncing India rubber ball, used for the first recorded indoor game in Montreal's Victoria Ice Rink in the late 1800s, broke $300 worth of windows before it was replaced with the rubber puck. Legend has it that the arena manager had the ball's rounded edges chopped off for the next game, making the first flat puck.

Today, the NHL puck is black, vulcanized (or weatherproof) rubber. It must be one inch thick, three inches in diameter, and weigh between five and a half and six ounces. The NHL crest appears on one side, and the home team's crest on the other.

Sticks

The heavy, one-piece wood stick is now a museum display. The modern hockey player's stick is usually made of aluminum, graphite, fibreglass, or other "composite" materials, allowing players to shoot much harder. Some sticks allow for the replacement of the blade.

continued from page 23

1950-1959

Facts on the Fly

The Refereeing Life

Officiating today is much different from what it was long ago when a referee rang a bell to end a play — the cold metal of a whistle would freeze to his lips outdoors or in a cold arena.

Today, the NHL has about 45 full-time referees and 35 linesmen who officiate the 1,230 league games — plus exhibitions, playoffs, and the annual All-Star Game. All of them began in minor hockey as players or officials, and worked their way up to the NHL through junior hockey and North America's minor professional leagues.

Roy Alvin (Red) Storey, a native of Barrie, Ontario, was probably the most famous NHL referee of all, one of more than a dozen referees and linesmen who have been inducted into the Hockey Hall of Fame.

Storey was an athlete who had many talents, a fine hockey, baseball, football, and lacrosse player. He first became a star in the Canadian Football League, winning the Grey Cup with the Toronto Argonauts in 1937 and '38.

But he became just as famous as a referee in the NHL, joining the league in 1950 to wear the traditional shirt, tie, and sweater of an official. It wasn't until 1955, when games were televised, that referees wore the familiar black-and-white striped shirts that they still do today, so they'd be better seen by viewers.

Storey remained active in hockey long after he retired as a referee in 1959, working as a radio and TV commentator and as an entertaining speaker at sports banquets from coast to coast. He was mourned by all of Canada when he died at age 88 in March 2006.

Hall of Fame referee Red Storey (right), always in charge.
RED STOREY COLLECTION

The 1950s featured particularly fierce rivalries between teams that played each other 14 times every season in a 70-game schedule.

It wasn't uncommon for two clubs to play a rough, tough game in one city one night, then take the same train together to the other team's city and play each other again the following night. The emotions sometimes spilled into fighting, a part of hockey that is enjoyed by some fans and is a turnoff for others.

Fans packed the 1950s Montreal Forum all the way to the roof, and sometimes behind steel posts.
AUTHOR'S COLLECTION

Referees and linesmen became known as "zebras" for the striped sweaters they began wearing in the NHL in 1955.

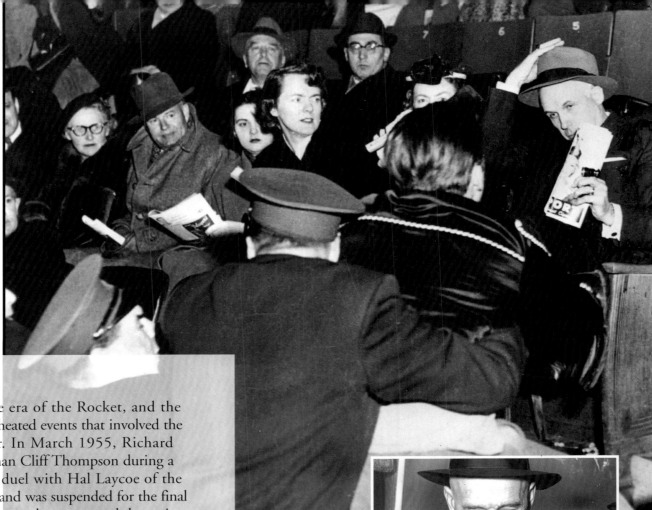

Ushers hold back a fan trying to attack NHL President Clarence Campbell at the Forum on March 17, 1955. Minutes later, the infamous Richard riot was underway.
CLASSIC COLLECTIBLES

This was the era of the Rocket, and the 1950s saw two heated events that involved the Canadiens star. In March 1955, Richard punched linesman Cliff Thompson during a stick-swinging duel with Hal Laycoe of the Boston Bruins, and was suspended for the final few games of the regular season and the entire playoffs by NHL President Clarence Campbell.

The battle with Thompson and Laycoe was bad enough. But Montreal fans were furious about Richard's punishment, and on March 17, with Campbell in attendance at the Forum, they rioted in the arena. Police cleared the building and fans spilled outside, causing huge damage in the streets. Montreal was forced to forfeit the game to Detroit.

Canadiens coach Dick Irvin Sr. holds the tear-gas canister that exploded at the Forum, starting the riot.
DICK IRVIN JR. COLLECTION

TIMELINE

1956
Canadiens' great Jean Béliveau is the first hockey player on the cover of *Sports Illustrated*.

1954
Fred Sasakamoose becomes the first full-blooded native Canadian in the NHL.

1952
Canada's first TV network, CBC, begins broadcasting.

1950
Each team must have an emergency goalie in the stands, ready to play in case their starting goalie is injured or ill.

1954
Teams agree to wear coloured uniforms at home and white uniforms on the road.

1951
The goal crease is increased from 3 x 7 feet to 4 x 8 feet.

1956
A player serving a minor penalty is allowed to return to the ice when the other team scores.

RULES

French broadcaster René Lecavalier behind his microphone.
LIBRARY AND ARCHIVES CANADA

Bernie (Boom Boom) Geoffrion smiles for a fan during a Canadiens Stanley Cup parade in the 1950s.
COURTESY JUDITH TOPOLNISKI

Facts on the Fly

Hockey Night in Canada

The 1950s marked the beginning of hockey on TV, with French broadcaster René Lecavalier announcing games on TV from the Montreal Forum and, soon afterward, Foster Hewitt doing the play-by-play in English from Toronto's Maple Leaf Gardens.

Hockey Night in Canada — La Soirée du Hockey in French — gave fans and their families something new to look forward to. The activities of an entire week were often planned around being home to watch the Saturday-night hockey game.

Since 1980, former NHL coach Don Cherry of Kingston, Ontario, has been a popular feature on the English telecast. In his first-intermission segment Coach's Corner, which he has done since 1987 alongside Ron MacLean, Cherry has both entertained and enraged fans with his shocking opinions and bright jackets and neckties. Fans either love Cherry, or love to hate him.

A little-known fact about Cherry is that he played in the NHL before he became a coach. He played one game on defence for the Boston Bruins in the 1954–55 season.

The Rocket lost the scoring title that season to his teammate, Bernie (Boom Boom) Geoffrion, so named for the booming slap shot he was perfecting. But Richard was back the following year, and led the Canadiens to their first of five straight Stanley Cup victories.

No other team has matched that achievement, and the club has won a record 24 Cups in all.

Ron MacLean (left) and Don Cherry on the TV set of *Hockey Night in Canada*'s Coach's Corner.
HOCKEY NIGHT IN CANADA

1960-1969

Hockey changed dramatically in the 1960s, when the NHL doubled in size from six to 12 teams for the 1967–68 season, seeking to open up new markets and create new fans in the United States. Joining the NHL were the Los Angeles Kings, Oakland Seals, Minnesota North Stars, Philadelphia Flyers, Pittsburgh Penguins, and St. Louis Blues.

With teams now on the West Coast, gone were the endless train rides players took between cities, often overnight. With travel across continents now involved, the airplane had become the only way to go.

The size of the league and the way teams got to their games were not the only things changing — equipment was taking new shape, as well, and a new type of stick was making a goalie's life miserable.

For many years a heavy, flat-bladed piece of wood, by the mid-1960s the hockey stick was now appearing with a huge curve in the blade.

Chicago's Bobby Hull and his Blackhawks teammate, Stan Mikita, were the first to bend big curves into their sticks, which caused their shots to rise very quickly from the ice, dipping and dancing unpredictably. Until 1967, there was no NHL rule to prevent bending the curve, and many a goalie had nightmares, bruises on his body, and stitches in his face from the hard, high shots of Hull, Mikita, and others.

It's a good thing that Jacques Plante had popularized the use of the face mask. Most goalies not wearing a mask soon were.

Young Chicago star Bobby Hull, nicknamed the Golden Jet, and his famous curved stick.
AUTHOR'S COLLECTION

Hull's teammate, Stan Mikita, here crowding Detroit goalie Roger Crozier, helped popularize the curved stick, too.
AUTHOR'S COLLECTION

TIMELINE

1961
Hockey Hall of Fame opens in Toronto.

1966
Bobby Orr signs a 2-year contract with Boston for $70,000, the NHL's best salary.

1965
Canada's red and white Maple Leaf flag is introduced, two years before the country's Centennial.

1964
Body contact on faceoffs is prohibited.

1965
Teams must dress two goalies.

1967
A player's stick must be curved no more than 1 1/2 inches, eliminating the "banana blade" curves. The curve is decreased to one inch in 1969, then to 1/2 inch a year later.

RULES

31

Legendary Canadiens captain Jean Béliveau hugs the Conn Smythe Trophy (left), the first time it was awarded to the most valuable player in the playoffs, and the Stanley Cup in 1965.
HOCKEY ONLINE

Facts on the Fly

Close To You

It wasn't until Nov. 8, 1963 that the NHL created separate penalty boxes for both teams. This happened for the first time in Toronto's Maple Leaf Gardens for a game between fierce rivals Toronto and the Montreal Canadiens. Before that, players sat shoulder-to-shoulder in one box, even after they had been penalized for fighting.

Toronto's Frank Mahovlich yells at a fan as he stands in the penalty box — right beside a Montreal player — during an early 1960s game.
LIBRARY AND ARCHIVES CANADA

One player who didn't need trick shots or a wildly curved stick was Canadiens captain Jean Béliveau.

Tall, strong, and a smooth skater who used an old-fashioned, almost straight blade, Béliveau was a skilled playmaker and stickhandler who had a dangerous backhand shot and could pass as easily as he could score.

In 1965, Béliveau was named winner of the first Conn Smythe Trophy, now presented annually to the most valuable player in the playoffs.

Chicago's Glenn Hall (right) introduced the butterfly style of goaltending (illustrated at left). It's the most popular style in the game today.

In the 1960s, team managers no longer assembled their teams based solely on where a young player lived or played. Beginning in 1963, the NHL's amateur "draft" put nearly all eligible players on a list, and the weakest teams made the first draft choices to get the most sought-after talent.

This gave them the best young players to strengthen their rosters, or allowed them to trade away that selection to bring an experienced player to their team immediately. This draft remains in effect today.

There hadn't been enough women playing hockey in Canada to fill a few teams, much less hold a draft. Their game had taken a long time to recover from World War II, when it was put on hold. But by the mid-1960s, Ontario and Quebec were forming female hockey programs, and others were following with programs of their own.

Bobby Orr (right) as captain of the junior-league Oshawa Generals in 1966, at age 18, celebrates a victory with teammates Danny O'Shea (left) and goalie Ian Young.
LIBRARY AND ARCHIVES CANADA

Facts on the Fly

They Called Him Mr. Goalie

Goalie Glenn Hall, who starred from 1955 to 1971 for the Detroit Red Wings, Chicago Blackhawks, and St. Louis Blues, used to be sick to his stomach before almost every game — a sign to others that he was very nervous, but a sign to Hall that he was as ready as he could be to play.

Mr. Goalie, as they called Hall, holds an NHL record that will never be broken: from 1955 to 1962, he played 502 games in a row. Including playoffs, his total was just short of 552 games. That's 33,135 minutes, or more than 6 1/2 full 82-game seasons without even one second off the ice.

The native of Humboldt, Saskatchewan, made about 16,000 saves during this stretch, and won the Stanley Cup with Chicago in 1961. His incredible streak ended in the 13th game of the 1962–63 season when he hurt his back while bending down to adjust a strap on his goalie pads. He had to leave the game in the second period, in too much pain to play.

1970-1979

Cold War

For about four decades after World War II, from roughly 1947 until the collapse of the Soviet Union and the so-called East Bloc of Eastern Europe, the world lived in a "Cold War."

While not traditional war with armies and tanks, the Cold War was a struggle that pitted the superpowers of the Soviet Union and the United States and their allies — or friendly partners — against each other in areas of economics and ideologies — or theories of government, social policy, and science.

It was a tense time that was reflected in the dramatic and historic 1972 Summit Series, the eight-game hockey series between Canada and the Soviets.

Facts on the Fly

A Goal To Sing About

Paul Henderson's winning goal in Game 8 of the Summit Series was so significant that, 26 years later, it made its way into a song recorded by the Canadian band The Tragically Hip. In the song "Fireworks," lead vocalist Gordon Downie sings, "If there's a goal that everyone remembers, it was back in ol' '72..."

In September 1972, every hockey fan was talking about the historic match between an all-star team of Canadian players and a squad of Russians.

It was called the Summit Series, in which four games were to be played in Canada, then four in Moscow. No one thought the Russians would win even a single game — except, of course, the Russians.

It was a highly emotional series that pitted our style of hockey — even our system of government and way of life — against that of the Soviets, who were regular champions in the international amateur games and the Olympics. The Summit Series would be nothing less than a war on ice.

Pierre Trudeau, then Canadian Prime Minister, dropped the ceremonial faceoff at the Montreal Forum on September 2, 1972, to begin the series. Players shook hands, exchanged pins in a sign of sportsmanship, and then Canada scored just 30 seconds into the game, and added another goal at 6:32 of the first period.

Prime Minister Pierre Trudeau drops the ceremonial faceoff between Team Canada's Phil Esposito (right) and Soviet Vladimir Starshinov.
DENIS BRODEUR

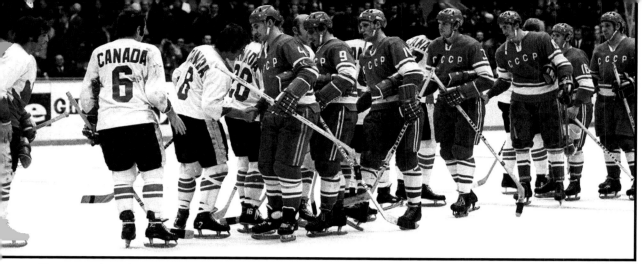

No matter how intense and heated the action on the ice during the historic series, players shook hands at the end of the games, as they did here in Moscow.
DENIS BRODEUR

But the Russians rallied. They didn't panic and they used their superb fitness to their advantage, winning the first game 7-3. It was a stunning defeat not just for our hockey team, but for our entire country.

Canada bounced back two nights later in Toronto, winning 4-1, then tied Game 3 in Winnipeg 4-4 — there was no overtime in this series — and lost Game 4 in Vancouver 5-3.

The series then moved to Moscow after a two-week break, and the Russians earned a 5-4 win in Game 5. Canada needed to win the next three games to win the series, a nearly impossible task, but they did so with victories of 3-2, 4-3, and 6-5.

Paul Henderson, a member of the Toronto Maple Leafs, became a national hero by scoring the winning goals in the final two games, his Game 8 winner coming with just 34 seconds left to play.

Team Canada hero Paul Henderson celebrates his winning goal in Game 8, jumping into the arms of teammate Yvan Cournoyer (No. 12), in front of fallen Soviet goalie Vladislav Tretiak and his two unhappy defencemen.
DENIS BRODEUR

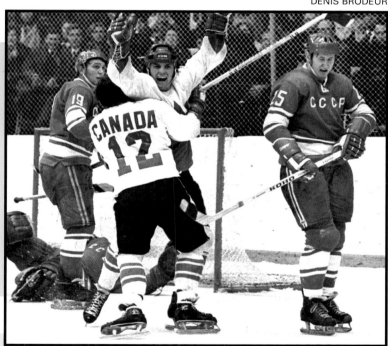

Globe and Mail,
September 29, 1972

TIMELINE

1977
NHL players must have their names on their sweaters.

1976
The death penalty is abolished in Canada.

1972
Canada beats Soviet Union in historic Summit Series.

1970
Home teams are to wear white sweaters, while visitors wear coloured sweaters.

1976
A major penalty and game misconduct will be given to any player deemed to be the aggressor in a fight.

1979
Any player now entering the NHL must wear a helmet.

RULES

Gerry Cheevers, a Hall of Fame goalie from St. Catharines, Ontario, won Stanley Cups with the Boston Bruins in 1970 and 1972. He used a felt pen to draw stitches on his mask to show where he'd have been cut for real.
CLASSIC COLLECTIBLES

This decade saw important accomplishments for Canadian hockey players. Forward Phil Esposito, the inspirational leader of Team Canada, and defenceman Bobby Orr, both natives of Ontario, led the Boston Bruins to two Stanley Cup victories in the 1970s. Orr was by far the best defenceman of his generation, if not of all time. More amazing is the fact that he played most of his 11-year NHL career on a terrible left knee, which was surgically repaired many times.

Facts on the Fly

The Hockey Song

There is one great country tune that will always get hockey fans humming along. It's called "The Hockey Song," and it was written and first recorded in 1973 by "Stompin'" Tom Connors of Saint John, New Brunswick.

The song had little popularity for nearly 20 years, until the Ottawa Senators began playing it at their home games. Pat Burns, then coach of the Toronto Maple Leafs and a huge fan of country music, insisted the Leafs play it, too.

Soon it spread far and wide, and you can't go to an NHL game today and not expect to hear it at some point.

Boston's Bobby Orr played most of his brilliant career in great pain. He was also the first NHL player to sign a million-dollar contract.

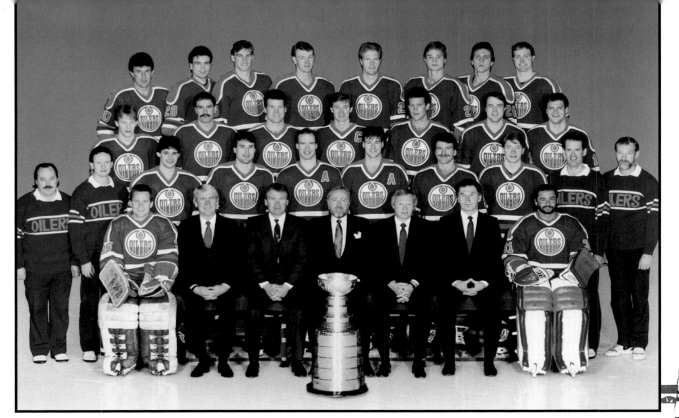

The Edmonton Oilers were a powerhouse in the 1980s, winning the Stanley Cup five times.
HOCKEY ONLINE

Goalie Ken Dryden went from the Canadiens net to the Hockey Hall of Fame to the House of Commons in Ottawa, where he was elected as a Liberal Member of Parliament.

The NHL hadn't had any serious competition since it was born in 1917, but that would change in 1972 when two American promoters created the 12-team World Hockey Association. Canadian teams in the WHA included Edmonton, Winnipeg, Toronto, Ottawa, and Quebec.

But within a few years the WHA was struggling financially and there was increasing talk of the league merging with the NHL. That finally happened after the 1978–79 season, seven years after the WHA had begun play. The Quebec Nordiques, Hartford Whalers, Winnipeg Jets, and Edmonton Oilers joined the NHL for the 1979–80 season.

Playing centre for Edmonton was a skinny 18-year-old from Brantford, Ontario, named Wayne Gretzky, who eight years earlier had scored 378 goals and 139 assists in one season of minor-league hockey, an incredible feat.

He had dominated the WHA with his brilliant play, so the hockey world asked, would this young man be as good in the NHL? Time was to prove the answer was yes.

Facts on the Fly

Skating Into Politics

Political office has long been a part of many NHL players' lives, after and even during their careers on ice.

Former Canadiens goalie Ken Dryden was elected to the House of Commons as a Member of Parliament for the Liberal Party in 2004 and 2006. Frank Mahovlich, Dryden's former teammate and a one-time Toronto Maple Leafs star, was appointed to the Senate in 1998.

Other players who ran for political office included Syl Apps, Howie Meeker, Bucko McDonald, Lionel Conacher, Red Kelly, Bill Hicke, and Dick Duff.

1980-1989

Wayne Gretzky will always be remembered for his amazing accomplishments as an Edmonton Oiler, especially his record 92 goals in 1981–82 and 163 assists in 1985–86.

Wayne Gretzky would completely rewrite the record books during an NHL career that spanned two decades.

Gretzky became the dominant player of his time largely because he had a knack of being not where the puck was, but where it was going to be.

He was soon nicknamed "The Great One" — he holds nearly every scoring record in the NHL, won the Hart Trophy nine times as the league's most valuable player, and 10 times won the Art Ross Trophy as the NHL's top point-scorer. Five times he won the Lady Byng Trophy as the most gentlemanly player in the league.

On February 24, 1980, Gretzky became the first NHL player to score 100 points in a season before he turned 20. It took him just 61 games to do it.

Gretzky led the Edmonton Oilers to four Stanley Cups in the mid-1980s, and retired in 1999 with 894 regular-season goals in 1,487 games, another 122 goals scored in 208 playoff games.

His trade to the Los Angeles Kings on August 9, 1988, was front-page news in every newspaper in Canada and many in the U.S.

Gretzky played eight seasons in Los Angeles, bringing a whole new generation of fans to hockey across the United States and creating much-needed NHL support south of the border.

The intense Mark Messier, nicknamed Moose, was the heart and soul of many great Oilers teams.
CP IMAGES/Ryan Remiorz

The sight of the Canadiens' Guy Lafleur racing down the ice terrorized many goalies in the 1970s and '80s.

Gordie Howe (below left) made history playing with his sons, Marty and Mark, with the Houston Aeros of the WHA and the Hartford Whalers of the NHL.
HOCKEY ONLINE

Other significant players and accomplishments were sometimes lost in Gretzky's shadow during the 1980s.

Bryan Trottier, born to an Irish mother and Cree/Chippewa father in Val Marie, Saskatchewan, and Montrealer Mike Bossy, one of the most natural goal-scorers ever, led the New York Islanders to four straight Stanley Cups from 1980–83.

Guy Lafleur of Thurso, Quebec, remained a bright light for the Canadiens, for whom he had been brilliant through the 1970s. Lafleur was nicknamed The Flower — the English translation of Lafleur — he was the most exciting player of his generation, his long hair flying behind him as he streaked down the right wing. He scored 560 goals in his 1,127 NHL games, and in his 13 seasons with the Canadiens, his team never once missed the playoffs.

There were other superb players during the "Gretzky era," including his teammates Mark Messier, Jari Kurri, and Paul Coffey; Marcel Dionne of Los Angeles; Peter Stastny of Quebec; Winnipeg's Dale Hawerchuk; Boston's Raymond Bourque; and the pesky, hard-skating, rough-and-tumble Doug Gilmour, who played on seven NHL clubs during his career and was adored by fans — as long as he played on their team.

Facts on the Fly

Like Father, Like Sons

NHL Hall of Fame legend Gordie Howe of Floral, Saskatchewan, made history at the age of 51 on March 9, 1980 when he played one shift on a line with his sons, Marty, age 26, and Mark, 24, for the Hartford Whalers. It was the first time, and surely the last, that a father and his two boys have played on one line in an NHL game.

TIMELINE

1981
Aluminum sticks are first used in the NHL.

1980
NHL legends Gordie Howe, Bobby Hull, and Stan Mikita retire.

1984
Marc Garneau is the first Canadian in space.

1988–89
Mario Lemieux scores 199 points this season.

1981
If both of a team's goalies are injured or otherwise unfit to play, the team can use any eligible goalie who is available.

1982
Teams are to dress 18 skaters and two goaltenders.

1983
Sudden-death overtime period of five minutes will follow all regular-season ties.

RULES

1990-1999

Facts on the Fly

Sledge Hockey

Sledge hockey is a fast, exciting sport played by athletes with a physical disability in their lower body that does not allow them to play traditional hockey.

The most basic rule is the same as in ice hockey — put the puck in your opponent's net — but the way to do so is quite different. Six players per team, including the goalie, are strapped into frames of metal that are attached to two normal skate blades. Each player uses two sticks, with spikes on one end to move up and down the ice, and stick blades on the other to shoot the puck.

The game was invented in 1961 by three Swedish wheelchair athletes, and since 1994 has become one of the most popular events at the Paralympic Winter Games, a global event held for physically-challenged athletes after each Winter Olympics.

Both women and men play the game, but only the men compete at the Paralympics. The Canadian team won the gold medal at the 2006 Paralympics in Turin, Italy, the silver in 1998, and the bronze in 1994. In addition, Canada won the 2000 world championship.

Team Canada's Jean Labonté, Hervé Lord, and Shawn Matheson, sledge hockey gold medalists at the 2006 Paralympic Games in Turin, Italy.
HOCKEY CANADA

The 1980s had closed with the Pittsburgh Penguins' Mario Lemieux scoring 199 points in 1988–89. It was the closest anyone had come to Wayne Gretzky's four seasons of 205 points or more during the '80s.

The native of Montreal captained the Penguins to their first Stanley Cup in 1991, having arrived in Pittsburgh seven years earlier as the first player chosen in the NHL draft. Lemieux then spoke barely a word of English, and yet was expected to lead the American team as the great talent everyone believed he was.

But it wasn't to be the biggest challenge of Lemieux's life. "Super Mario," as he was called, faced a tougher opponent than any who wore skates. In 1993, two seasons after leading the Penguins to the championship, he successfully fought Hodgkin's disease — a cancer of the lymph nodes. Lemieux inspired other cancer patients, and made regular visits to hospitals to meet sick children.

At the same time, another Quebecer was making headlines in the NHL — behind a goalie mask. You couldn't tell it was a woman in goal for the Tampa Bay Lightning in their September 1992 exhibition game against the St. Louis Blues, but Manon Rhéaume of Lac Beauport, Quebec, made history as the first female to play in a game between two NHL teams, facing nine shots and giving up two goals.

TIMELINE

1999
Wayne Gretzky — The Great One — retires.

1998
Huge ice storm leaves millions without electricity in Ontario and Quebec.

1994
Sports Act declaring hockey as Canada's national winter sport is passed.

1991
Video replay is used to help referees decide goal/no goal situations.

A goal does not count if an attacking player's skate is in the crease.

1999
Teams play with four skaters and a goalie during regular-season overtime.

RULES

Manon Rhéaume won a 1998 Olympic silver medal for Canada in Nagano, Japan. Six years earlier, she played in an NHL exhibition game.
CP IMAGES/COC

Colorado goalie Patrick Roy stands in his net, surrounded by dozens of rubber rats thrown by Florida fans.
CP IMAGES/Rick Bowmer

In 1990, women were playing for their first world championship, and Canada beat the U.S. for that historic title in Ottawa.

Later, in 1998, NHL players were allowed to compete in the Nagano Olympics in Japan. The Czech Republic won the men's tournament, while the U.S. shocked Canada by winning the women's gold medal.

If Olympic participation was a highlight, a dark spot was a labour dispute during the 1994–95 season that cancelled 468 games. Owners of the NHL teams "locked out" the players for 104 days in a disagreement over a contract between the two sides.

When play resumed on January 11, 1995, the season was shortened from 84 to 48 games. Among the issues was a "salary cap" — a maximum amount of money each team's players would be paid. Ten years later, that same issue would wipe out the entire 2004–05 season.

The 1990s gave us faster and stronger players, many of them Europeans who brought their speed and skill to North America. The European game promotes more skating, as it's played on a surface 200 feet long by 100 feet wide — 15 feet wider than an NHL rink.

NHL teams began hiring strength and conditioning coordinators to help improve the fitness of all players.

A "Rat Trick" in Florida:

A live rat raced through the Florida Panthers' dressing room on October 8, 1995, and was swatted by Florida player Scott Mellanby, a native of Montreal. That night, Mellanby scored two goals, and Panthers goalie John Vanbiesbrouck called it a "rat trick."

The story spread, and soon fans were tossing rubber rats onto the ice any time the Panthers scored. By the time the playoffs rolled around, more than 2,000 rats were raining out of the stands, and the visiting goalie would sometimes crawl into his net to avoid being hit.

Facts on the Fly

In 1945, the term *"hat trick"* was used for a three-goal performance by a player in a single game. A Toronto tailor in the 1940s would give Maple Leafs players a new hat if they scored three goals in one game. Since then, fans have showered the ice with hats when a player from the home team scores three times. The hats are usually given to local charities.

Facts on the Fly

Ottawa Senators Welcomed Back in NHL

Many hockey fans today don't realize that the Ottawa Senators have long been Stanley Cup champions. The Senators won Cups in 1920, '21, '23, and '27. But they ran out of money during the Great Depression of the 1930s, took a season off in 1931–32, then moved to St. Louis after the 1933–34 season, becoming known as the Eagles. The team that had made history on February 11, 1922 playing the NHL's first-ever tie game against Toronto shut down after one more year.

The Senators returned for the 1992–93 season, paying $50 million for another NHL franchise.

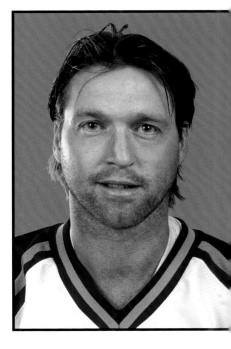

Quebec City native Patrick Roy, a superstar with the Montreal Canadiens and Colorado Avalanche, retired in 2003 holding NHL goaltending records for career victories (551), games played (1,029), playoff victories (151), and playoff games played (247).
NHL

1992 OTTAWA SENATORS 1993

The league welcomed its next flock of superstars during the 1990s. Some had arrived earlier, but players like Brett Hull, Steve Yzerman, Jaromir Jagr, and Joe Sakic, and goalies like Patrick Roy, Martin Brodeur, and Dominik Hasek were impressive throughout the decade.

These players, and hundreds more, were at fans' fingertips in new waves of hockey cards and on dozens of computer hockey games.

Canadians no longer were relying merely on television and newspapers to keep track of their favourite teams. The internet, which came about during this time, was doing a good job of that, too, something Lord Stanley of Preston had never dreamed 100 years earlier.

And in 1999, The Great One retired from the New York Rangers, his fourth NHL club, and hung up his skates for good. When Gretzky ended his career, the NHL announced that no player on any team would ever again wear the No. 99 he had made famous.

But Gretzky wasn't gone from hockey — he would soon return to the game as general manager of Canada's victorious men's team at the 2002 Salt Lake Olympic Winter Games, the World Cup of Hockey, and would later become part-owner and coach of the NHL's Phoenix Coyotes.

The internet let fans follow the game like never before. They got to study the 1992–93 Ottawa Senators, back in the NHL after having been gone for nearly 60 years.
HOCKEY ONLINE

2000 & BEYOND

With Wayne Gretzky assembling the team, Canada won the men's gold medal at the 2002 Salt Lake Olympics with a thrilling 5-2 victory over the United States. It was Canada's first Olympic hockey gold in 50 years.

Three days earlier, the Canadian women's team had also beaten the U.S. 3-2 for the gold. This was sweet revenge for the women's team, which had lost to the Americans at Nagano in 1998. Canada's women's team featured excellent veteran players like captain Cassie Campbell, Thérèse Brisson, Danielle Goyette, and Geraldine Heaney.

It was later learned that Edmonton's Trent Evans, the man responsible for making the ice in Salt Lake's hockey arena, had buried a Canadian one-dollar coin beneath centre ice. This "loonie," which is thought to have brought luck to Canada, is now on display at the Hall of Fame in Toronto.

Facts on the Fly

Canada Rules the NHL

Even if the Canadian men's team was thumped at the Turin Olympics, our country can still take pride in this impressive fact: of the league's 710 players on opening-game rosters for the 2005–06 season, 371 players, or 52.3 percent, were from Canada. That was down from the 78.3 percent in 1983–84, when there were far fewer American- and European-born players in the NHL. Canada continues to provide more players to the NHL than any other country.

Team Canada's Caroline Ouellette (left) and Kim St-Pierre celebrate their gold-medal victory at the 2006 Turin Olympic Winter Games.
CP IMAGES/Gene J. Puskar

TIMELINE

2005
Michaëlle Jean is named Canada's 27th Governor-General, the 21st since Lord Stanley of Preston.

2004–05
Entire NHL season is wiped out by a labour dispute.

2003
First outdoor game in NHL history, the Heritage Classic, is played in front of 57,167 fans at Edmonton's Commonwealth Stadium in -30°C weather.

2000
Two referees to be used for all games.

2003
Home teams again wear coloured uniforms; visiting teams wear basic white sweaters.

2005
A major rule package is introduced, including shootouts to decide regular-season games if tied after overtime, goalie pads reduced to 11 inches from 12, and the red line eliminated to allow for two-line passes.

RULES

Behind The Bench

Usually, a hockey team is only as good as its coach. Without good strategy played by effective lines, who are directed by a coach with the skills and experience to plan the attack, make changes during a game, and motivate his players, a team will not win a championship.

In the NHL, William Scott (Scotty) Bowman was the winner of a record nine Stanley Cups and is the only coach in North American pro baseball, basketball, football, or hockey to win titles with three different teams.

Bowman won 1,244 regular-season games and 243 more in the playoffs during more than 30 years of coaching five NHL teams. He won five Stanley Cups behind the bench of the Montreal Canadiens in the 1970s, another with the Pittsburgh Penguins in 1992, and three more with the Detroit Red Wings, in 1997, '98, and 2002, before he retired.

In the earlier days, a coach worked alone, and sometimes also was general manager of his team, scouting talent and signing players to contracts. There were many great coaches — Dick Irvin Sr. in Toronto, Montreal, and Chicago; Toe Blake in Montreal and Punch Imlach in Toronto; Jack Adams in Detroit, for whom the Jack Adams Award has been awarded since 1974 to the NHL's outstanding coach; and Billy Reay in Chicago.

Coaching has become a science at all levels. Today, NHL coaches work with several assistants, some even high in the press box, communicating with the bench by two-way radio. They also have the advantage of using videotape and TV satellites to watch other teams and plan strategies.

Today's minor-hockey coaches, both men and women, study special courses designed to teach them the finest points of hockey. The vast majority are unpaid volunteers, working simply for the love of the game and the appreciation of the players they coach.

Globe and Mail,
March 11, 2005

Clarkson to reward women's champion

With women's hockey in the Olympics, interest in the game in Canada was growing faster than ever. There were more opportunities for girls and women to play hockey, with teams springing up in every province and territory. In 2005, retiring Governor-General Adrienne Clarkson donated the Clarkson Cup, to be awarded annually for excellence in women's hockey.

In the year 2000, the NHL welcomed back one of its best talents. Mario Lemieux returned to the game in December after quitting in 1997 and being elected to the Hall of Fame. He played a significant role in Team Canada's Olympic victory in Salt Lake City, bought the NHL's Pittsburgh Penguins, and became the league's dominant forward as that team's captain.

In Montreal, Canadiens captain Saku Koivu soon would be going through a cancer battle, and like Lemieux, he too would return to the ice. Koivu came back a stronger hockey player and as a leader on the NHL's most successful team, and by now one that was rebuilding for the future.

The beginning of this decade made many NHL players wealthy beyond their wildest dreams. In 2003–04, the average NHL salary for a player was $1,830,126 — $1 million more than it was in 1994. This became a strain on team owners.

Scotty Bowman is the most successful coach in NHL history, winning nine Stanley Cups while coaching three teams. He was a fine junior player as a youth, seen with the Montreal junior Royals in 1954.
NHL; AUTHOR'S COLLECTION

Super Mario, slowed by nagging injuries, retired for good in late January 2006, at the age of 40.

Cancellation of the 2004-05 season angered and saddened fans.

By comparison, the salaries of all players combined on an NHL team in 1925 could not be more than $35,000. In 1933, the "salary cap" for a team was $62,500, and no player could earn more than $7,000.

On September 16, 2004, without a contract with their players who wanted more money than the owners were willing to pay, the NHL locked them out for the second time in 10 years. This lockout lasted 301 days and cancelled 1,230 games — the entire 2004–05 season.

To earn money and keep fit in case the dispute ended suddenly, nearly 400 NHL players joined teams with 19 leagues in Europe.

Owners and players talked for months and finally agreed to a new six-year contract — a collective bargaining agreement — on July 22, 2005.

The major issue was a salary cap, which for the first year meant a team's total salaries could be no higher than $39 million (U.S.). Today, the smallest annual salary paid in the NHL is $450,000 (U.S.) — almost 13 times the amount a 1925 team was allowed to pay ALL of its players — and the highest is $7.8 million.

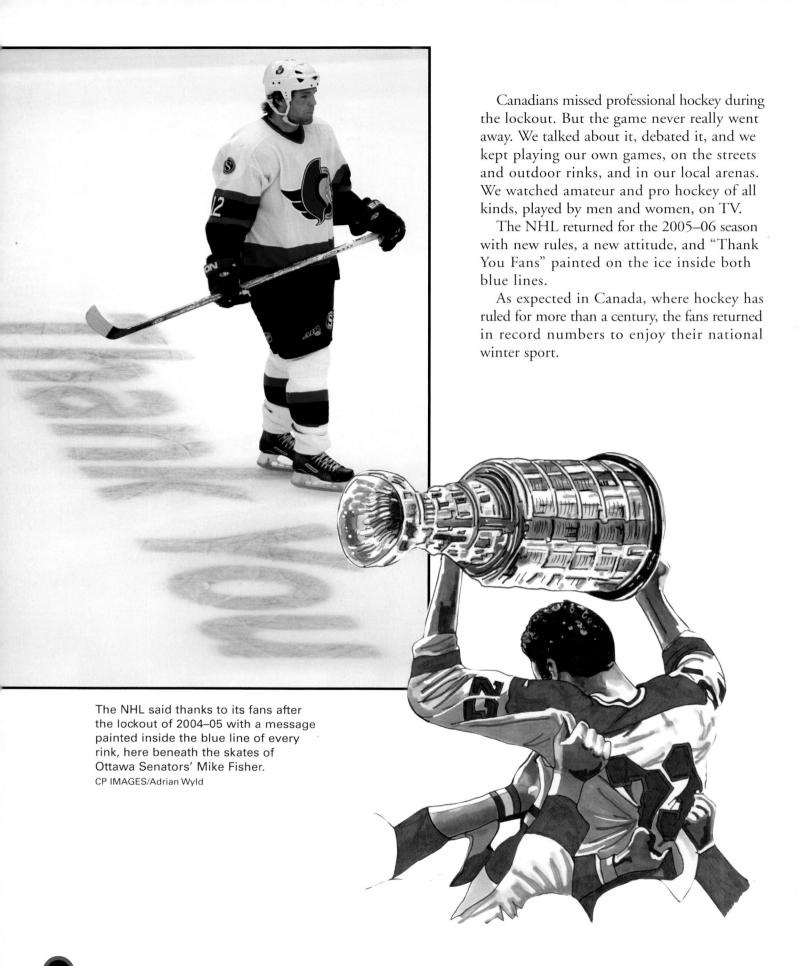

Canadians missed professional hockey during the lockout. But the game never really went away. We talked about it, debated it, and we kept playing our own games, on the streets and outdoor rinks, and in our local arenas. We watched amateur and pro hockey of all kinds, played by men and women, on TV.

The NHL returned for the 2005–06 season with new rules, a new attitude, and "Thank You Fans" painted on the ice inside both blue lines.

As expected in Canada, where hockey has ruled for more than a century, the fans returned in record numbers to enjoy their national winter sport.

The NHL said thanks to its fans after the lockout of 2004–05 with a message painted inside the blue line of every rink, here beneath the skates of Ottawa Senators' Mike Fisher.
CP IMAGES/Adrian Wyld

QUIZ

TWENTY QUESTIONS

Let's see if you've been paying close attention.
Answers to every question in the quiz below can be found in this book:

1. To whom was the hockey trophy donated by Canada's sixth Governor-General, Lord Stanley of Preston, first awarded ?

2. Most evidence suggests that hockey was born in which city?

3. Where did the rules of hockey first appear?

4. Who is the goal net said to have been invented by?

5. The first goalie pads were patterned after those worn in which sport?

6. Which team was the National Hockey League's first champion?

7. Why were the Stanley Cup playoffs of 1919 cancelled?

8. During which year did hockey first appear in the Olympic Games?

9. How much did the most expensive ticket to an NHL game in 1927–28 cost?

10. Which Canadian hockey announcer became famous for yelling, "He shoots! He scores!" after a team had scored a goal?

11. Who was Maurice (Rocket) Richard's centreman on the Montreal Canadiens' famous Punch Line in the 1940s?

12. Where did the first hockey cards appear?

13. Who was the first goalie known to have worn a mask in a game?

14. Why did women's hockey largely disappear in Canada for about 25 years?

15. Icemaker Trent Evans of Edmonton buried something beneath centre ice in Salt Lake City

that was said to bring Canada luck to win the men's and women's 2002 Olympic hockey gold medals. What did he bury?

16. Who was the first woman to appear in a game between two NHL teams?

17. Which Canadian singer recorded "The Hockey Song," a catchy tune played at arenas throughout the NHL?

18. Which Canadian player was the Game 8 hero of the 1972 Summit Series between Canada and the Soviet Union?

19. What objects were used as a "puck" during the early days of hockey?

20. Mario Lemieux of the Pittsburgh Penguins and Saku Koivu of the Montreal Canadiens both returned to hockey after treatment for what?

ANSWERS

1. Canada's best amateur team 2. Montreal, Quebec 3. In a newspaper: the *Montreal Gazette* 4. Two goalies 5. Cricket 6. Toronto Arenas 7. Because of an outbreak of the Spanish Influenza 8. 1920 9. $3.50 10. Foster Hewitt 11. Elmer Lach 12. On cigarette packages. 13. Elizabeth Graham 14. World War II 15. A one-dollar loonie coin 16. Manon Rhéaume 17. Stompin' Tom Connors 18. Paul Henderson 19. A flattened tin can, frozen horse manure, a rubber ball, wooden pucks, frozen fruit 20. Cancer.

47

HOCKEY *from* A *to* Z

All-star – A player who is among the best of the best. In the NHL, he's invited to play in the annual all-star game.

Backchecker – A forward who skates deep into his own zone to check an opponent off the puck or prevent him from getting a scoring chance.

Change on the fly – When a coach substitutes players while the game continues.

Deflection – A redirection of the puck, accidental or intentional, after a shot or pass has been made.

Empty-net goal – A goal scored into an undefended goal, usually in the dying minutes of a game, when the losing team has pulled its goalie for an extra attacker.

Five hole – The space between a goalie's pads.

Give and go – When one player passes the puck to a teammate, skates into the open, and receives a pass from the player to whom he has just passed.

Hat trick – Three goals scored by one player. If the player scores three goals uninterrupted by teammates' or opponents' scores, it's called a natural hat trick.

Ice time – Minutes played by a skater in a game.

Judge of play – A second referee who was used in games of the 1910s and 1920s; today, the NHL uses two referees in all games.

Killing a penalty – Preventing the opposition from scoring while they are on a power-play.

Linesman – Striped-shirt official who watches for icing, offsides and some infractions, and drops most faceoffs.

Minor – A two-minute penalty.

Neutral zone – The area between the blue lines.

One-timer – A shot, usually a slap shot, taken immediately after receiving a pass, without stopping the puck and setting up.

Playmaker – A player whose greatest skill is passing the puck and setting up scoring chances.

Quinella – Scoring all five types of goal in a single game: even-strength, power play, shorthanded, penalty shot, and empty net. Pittsburgh Penguins' Mario Lemieux did this on New Year's Eve 1988 vs. the New Jersey Devils.

Rebound – A puck that caroms off the goalie back into play after a save.

Slot – The area directly in front of the net, from the crease to the top of the faceoff circles.

Top shelf – The upper part of the net, under the crossbar. When a shooter whips the puck into the net here, it is said that "he went top shelf."

Underdog – The team that is expected to lose a game.

Visor – A transparent plastic face guard, attached to the front of the helmet, to protect the eyes.

Weak side – The side of the offensive or defensive zone where the fewest number of players are positioned.

X-ray – A medical image taken by doctors to determine whether an injured player has a broken bone.

Yeremeyev – Goalie Vitali Yeremeyev of Kazakhstan, one of the best tongue-twisting names to ever play in the NHL. (Say it fast three times!)

Zebra – Slang for a referee or linesman who wears a black-and-white striped shirt.

(Most terms courtesy of *Total Hockey, The Official Encyclopedia of the National Hockey League*)